Home-Made Ca

Authors' other books

HOME BAKED: A LITTLE BOOK OF BREAD RECIPES
(by George and Cecilia Scurfield)

Home-Made Cakes and Biscuits

by

George and Cecilia Scurfield

FABER AND FABER
3 Queen Square
London

First published in 1963
This edition published 1975
by Faber and Faber Limited
3 Queen Square London W.C.1
Reprinted 1977
Printed in Great Britain by
Jarrold and Sons Ltd, Norwich
All rights reserved

ISBN 0 571 10699 4

To
POLDI

NOTE

The 'I' in this book is Cecilia. My share in the making of this book has been solely clerical. G. S.

Contents

INTRODUCTION

Tea seems to be the meal which is most often ignored by connoisseurs of good food. Perhaps this is because afternoon tea is a feminine meal and many connoisseurs are men, or perhaps it is because you cannot drink wine at tea. . . . Whatever the reason, it seems to me to be a pity, because tea is the one meal which still retains, at its best, a distinctly British flavour and also because it is a meal at which the food is judged by much the same standards by people of all walks of life in this country. A menu saying 'home-made cakes, bread and jam' arouses the same expectations of excellence in us all, whereas one saying that 'the pâté is made by the proprietor himself' would leave many people cold. (That both notices might be equally misleading, does not alter the fact that more people would be aware that they had been misled by the first.)

Tea, in order to become a meal in its own right, must include a cake or cakes. A cup of tea and a slice of bread and butter or a biscuit is not a meal, it is a snack. No cake for tea is a dismal thing and reminiscent of juvenile punishments. Yet it is all too easy for a busy mother to produce her favourite cake so often that finally it grows stale long before it is finished. I have therefore included some recipes in this book which are economical or quick to prepare, or both, in the hope that something new can be put on the family table without too much trouble to the cook.

Apart from their function at tea, cakes can make an admirable finish for a luncheon or dinner. In their more exquisite versions they would not disgrace the most fastidious menu and they have the advantage for most hostesses of being preparable well in advance. It is a pity that some restaurants which excel at main dishes descend to tinned fruit and mass-produced ice-cream for dessert. They would do better to produce a really good cake which would round off the meal with a touch of individuality.

I have included some biscuits and pastries in this little book because very often the dividing line between them and cakes is hard to draw anyway. It is a pleasant contrast to have biscuits as well as cakes on the tea-table and a tin of home-made biscuits is always useful. Many of them keep admirably in an airtight tin and they are a stand-by for unexpected visitors or for days when there just isn't enough time to make a cake.

I have tried to divide the cakes into sections according to their main ingredients. Many people have their favourite flavours and it seems the simplest way for people to find what cake they can make with the ingredients in their store cupboard. However, as very many cakes are based on two basic recipes, the fatless sponge and the plain creamed mixture, I have given my favourite recipes for these two in the opening chapter, with a few suggestions on varying the flavour. The ingenious cook will, of course, be able to think of many more.

I would like to apologize to natives of those countries whose recipes I may have borrowed. Such delicate and delicious things undergo a sea change when they are produced by an alien cook. I can only plead that I've written them down here because the results have proved popular with my own family and friends and that they are the nearest I can get to the original.

1. BASIC CAKES

A great many cakes are variations on two basic methods: the fatless sponge and the plain creamed mixture.

Most people have their favourite recipe for a plain cake (the plain creamed mixture) and here is mine.

Ingredients:

> 6 oz. butter
> 6 oz. sugar
> 4 eggs
> 8 oz. flour
> 2 teaspoons baking powder
> pinch of salt
> milk to mix

Method:

Cream the fat and sugar together until they are really soft like whipped cream. This doesn't take very long if you cut up the butter and warm it first—but don't 'oil' the butter. Separate the whites and yolks of the eggs. Beat the yolks, one at a time, into the butter and sugar mixture. Sieve the flour, salt and baking powder together several times. If you want to mix in the baking powder properly this is really necessary. If you use a recipe in which cocoa and flour are sieved together you will see that several sievings are needed before the cocoa is evenly distributed, and the same applies to baking powder. Then whisk the egg whites until they are fairly firm but not stiff and dry, Fold the flour into the sugar, butter, egg mixture, and finally fold in the egg white and add enough milk to make a 'dropping mixture'—probably about half a teacupful. Try to avoid beating the mixture, just turn it gently, over and over, but flour, egg whites and milk should all be thoroughly mixed in. Put into a well-buttered cake tin—with greaseproof paper at the bottom, this will make it much easier to turn out—and bake in a moderate oven (300°) for about 1 hour.

Do use butter if you possibly can. It will only add a few pence on to the cost of the cake and it will make all the difference to the flavour. If not, use half butter and half margarine, or half margarine and half lard. Margarine by itself is often not 'fatty' enough.

Here is my basic recipe for a fatless sponge.

Ingredients:

    4 eggs
    the weight of the 4 eggs in castor or
      icing sugar
    the weight of 3 eggs in flour
    one tablespoon full of lemon juice or
      warm water

I use the eggs to weigh the other ingredients because proportions are important in a sponge and eggs vary in size.

Method:

Sieve the flour once or twice to make sure there are no lumps and that it is well aerated.

Separate the whites and the yolks of the eggs.

Beat the yolks of the eggs with the sugar until they become thick and pale in colour. This will take some time but it is very important not to stint your labours on this part of the operation!

Whisk the egg whites until they are stiff but not too dry.

Fold the flour bit by bit into the egg yolk, sugar mixture. Use a metal spoon and make sure there are no bits of dry flour left—but don't beat the mixture.

Fold in the egg whites, again making sure that they are thoroughly mixed in. Finally, stir in the lemon juice or hot water very gently.

The mixture should be spongy and yet fairly runny. Divide into sandwich tins which have been well greased and had castor sugar lightly shaken all over them—put a little sugar into each tin and shake it all over.

Bake in a fairly hot oven, 350° to 400°, for about 25 minutes.

A wire whisk is really the best thing to beat with because it does aerate the mixture better than a rotary whisk. I find this takes a long time so I cheat and start off with the rotary whisk and complete my beating with the wire one—this seems to work pretty well.

Both these recipes are open to as many variations as you have ideas, but remember, if you use other dry ingredients, like cocoa or ground almonds then you must subtract the weight of these ingredients from the amount of flour used.

As this is a chapter on basics I would like to add a note

on flavourings. Please try not to use so-called 'essences'! Lemon or orange flavouring is best got from the grated rinds of the fruits themselves. Vanilla pods give a far more delicate flavour than the commercial essence. They are rather expensive to buy, but do try them as they are not at all extravagant in use. Keep a jar of castor sugar and one of icing sugar with a vanilla pod buried in each. The pods will flavour the sugar and if you keep the jars filled up the pods will continue to do their job for many weeks.

If you do use commercial essences then please use them sparingly. Too much flavouring is worse than too little if your other ingredients are good.

Keep one or two miniature bottles of liqueurs in your store cupboard. Brandy and rum are especially useful. And then you can add a touch of luxury to otherwise plain cakes.

II. FRUIT CAKES

Cakes made with dried fruits are generally good keepers. Some of the richer ones are all the better for keeping. They are excellent for picnics as they are usually firm in texture and not sticky to eat.

Here is one of the favourites in our family. It is much more economical to make than many fruit cakes and it has a rather unusual flavour because of the demerara sugar. It is called:

Boodles Club Cake

Ingredients:
  ½ lb. butter
  ½ lb. demerara sugar
  ½ lb. raisins (sultanas will do but raisins give a better flavour)
  2 eggs
  1 lb. flour
  2 teaspoons bicarbonate of soda
  ¼ pint milk

Method:

Cream the butter and sugar. Beat in the eggs. Stir in the flour mixed with the dried fruit.

Dissolve the bicarbonate of soda in the milk which should be slightly warmed, and beat this mixture into the other ingredients and mix really well.

Bake in a moderate oven for about 3 hours in a lined tin.

This makes a large cake—but the quantities can easily be halved.

Economy Fruit Cake

This is a huge cake, economical to make and a good keeper. It isn't particularly luscious but it's just the thing if you are facing a week-end with lots of young people with hearty appetites. You need a very big tin to bake it in.

Ingredients:
- ½ pint sugar
- ½ pint melted butter or margarine
- ½ pint strong coffee
- 2 eggs
- 1 teaspoon mixed spice
- 1 cup sultanas
- grated rind of an orange
- 2 pints flour
- ½ pint golden syrup
- 2 level dessert spoons baking-powder

Method:

Beat up the eggs and sugar until pale and fluffy. Sift the flour and baking-powder together. Add all the ingredients to the eggs and sugar mixture, stirring in the flour and sultanas last. Turn into a large greased and floured tin (a 9″ cake-tin or a roasting-tin) and bake in a moderate oven (350°) for just under an hour.

Sponge Fruit Cake

This is much lighter than the average fruit cake.

Ingredients:
- 5 oz. seeded raisins
- 2 oz. shelled walnuts
- 7 oz. flour
- 1 teaspoon cinnamon
- 1 teaspoon lemon juice
- 4 oz. butter
- 7 oz. castor sugar
- yolks of 3 eggs and 1 white
- 1 level teaspoon bicarbonate of soda
- pinch of salt

Method:

Chop the raisins and walnuts coarsely. Put them in a basin and pour over them the bicarbonate of soda dissolved in a breakfast-cup full of boiling water. Leave them to stand while you sift the flour with the salt.

Cream the butter and sugar (if possible flavoured with vanilla). Beat the egg yolks and the white thoroughly and add them to the creamed mixture. Stir in the cinnamon and lemon juice and then stir in the flour alternately with the fruit and nuts. Do not beat but mix well.

Bake in a large loaf-tin in a very moderate oven (335° Regulo 3) for 1¼ hours. Cool in the tin for 5 minutes before turning it out.

Christmas Cake

This is the Christmas Cake I make every year for our family. None of us like icing so I just arrange some blanched almonds on the top of the cake before putting it in the oven. Make it several weeks before you need it. And if you do like icing start work on it two days before you intend to eat it.

Cover it with a layer of almond icing and cover this with a layer of water icing. When this is dry cover it with royal icing and allow this to dry overnight in a warm room before you start to decorate. Allow another twelve hours for the decorations to dry out, also. If you don't like almond icing, start with the water icing which will give a smooth surface to the cake.

Ingredients:

$\frac{3}{4}$ lb. butter
1 lb. sultanas
$\frac{1}{2}$ lb. chopped peel
1 lb. flour
1 lb. raisins
6 eggs
1 lb. sugar
$\frac{1}{2}$ lb. ground almonds
a little nutmeg and mixed spice
the juice of a lemon
$\frac{1}{2}$ wineglass brandy

Method:

Rub the butter into the flour and sugar, add the fruit and other dry ingredients. Beat the eggs and add them to the mixture with the brandy and the lemon juice. Mix very well. Line a 9″ tin and bake in a very slow oven for about 8 hours.

Bishops Bread

This is my version of the Austrian cake known as Bischofsbrot. It is extravagant but rich and very delicious. It is unusual in having grated chocolate in it.

Ingredients:

> 2 eggs, and their weight in butter, flour and sugar
> 2 oz. raisins
> 2 oz. almonds, or other nuts
> 2 oz. chocolate
> 2 oz. candied peel

Method:

Separate the egg yolks and whites. Chop the chocolate and nuts.

Cream the butter with half the sugar. Add the egg yolks and cream well.

Whisk the egg whites until stiff, then whisk in the rest of the sugar.

Fold the egg whites into the butter-sugar mixture alternately with the flour. Add the other ingredients gradually.

Bake in an oblong tin in a moderate oven (360° Regulo 4) for about 45 minutes.

French Plum Cake

Ingredients:

> 6 oz. sugar
> 6 oz. butter

       4 oz. seeded raisins
       2 oz. currants
       2 oz. mixed cut peel
       4 eggs
       11 oz. flour
       2 teaspoons baking-powder
       1 tablespoon rum

Method:

Cream the sugar and the butter. Add the dried fruit and the eggs, one by one. Beat well after adding each egg. Sift the flour and the baking-powder together and fold into the mixture. Add the rum and then beat thoroughly. Line a large bread-tin with waxed paper and fill it three-quarters full with the batter. Bake for 45 to 50 minutes in a warm oven, 375°, Regulo 4.

Scotch Seed Cake

Ingredients:

       $\frac{1}{2}$ lb. flour
       $\frac{1}{2}$ lb. butter
       $\frac{1}{2}$ lb. sugar
       2 oz. almonds (bitter if possible)
       4 oz. orange peel
       $2\frac{1}{2}$ oz. citron peel
       5 eggs
       $\frac{1}{2}$ a grated nutmeg
       $\frac{1}{2}$ teaspoon caraway seeds
       $\frac{1}{2}$ wineglass brandy

Method:

Cream the butter and sugar. Beat the eggs well and add them to the mixture bit by bit alternately with the flour.

Add all the other dry ingredients, except the caraway seeds, and finally, stir in the brandy. Pour into a well-lined cake-tin. Sprinkle the caraway seeds on top and bake in a moderate oven, 340°, Regulo 3. Avoid moving the cake until it is nearly done.

Dundee Cake

Ingredients:

> 10 oz. flour
> 4 oz. currants
> 4 oz. raisins
> 4 oz. sultanas
> 4 oz. mixed chopped peel
> 3 oz. ground almonds
> 2 oz. whole almonds
> grated rind of 1 orange
> 5 eggs
> 8 oz. butter
> 8 oz. sugar
> pinch of salt

Method:

Cream the butter and the sugar. Add the eggs and sieved flour alternately, beating well. Add the fruit, ground almonds, the grated orange rind, and the salt. Turn into a well-greased and lined tin. Cover the top with the almonds (which may be split first) and bake in a slow oven, 325°, Regulo 2, for 2½ hours.

III.
CHOCOLATE CAKES

Chocolate is one of the favourite cake flavours. It's well worth keeping some plain chocolate in your store cupboard for use in making cakes. These range from quite economical ones to the most extravagant and delicious concoctions. All of them are improved by being served with whipped cream. And chocolate goes very well with coffee so that any chocolate cake can be served as dessert.

If you have no plain chocolate in the house you can substitute cocoa in those recipes in which the chocolate is melted first. Mix the cocoa with a little milk and stir over heat into a smooth, thick paste. You will not need as much cocoa as chocolate—about half the quantity—and you may find you need a little more sugar—but this is a question of taste.

I start with a cake I make very often because it is quick and economical and also a good keeper. In fact, it improves if not cut for a day or two. It is called:

Chocolate Manitou

Ingredients:

>   3 oz. plain chocolate
>   1 teacup milk
>   1½ teacups flour
>   3 oz. butter
>   3 oz. sugar
>   1 egg
>   2 teaspoons baking-powder
>   1 teaspoon bicarbonate of soda
>   vanilla pod or essence

Method:

Melt the chocolate in the milk with a piece of vanilla pod and one ounce of the butter. Stir over a gentle heat until the chocolate is quite melted. Cut up the rest of the butter in a mixing-bowl and pour over the hot chocolate mixture after removing the vanilla pod. Stir until the butter has melted.

Then stir in the sugar and the egg. Beat in the flour and, lastly, add the baking-powder and the bicarbonate. Beat thoroughly—a wire whisk is best.

Pour into a well-greased tin and bake in a moderate oven, 350°, Regulo 4, for about 45 minutes.

(If you have no vanilla pod, add a half teaspoonful of vanilla essence when you put in the egg and the sugar.)

Devil's Food Cake

Ingredients:

>   ½ lb. flour
>   ½ teaspoon bicarbonate of soda
>   1½ teaspoons baking-powder
>   ½ lb. sugar

1 teaspoon salt
¼ lb. butter
4 tablespoons sour cream or milk
2 tablespoons hot milk
3 oz. chocolate
2 eggs
vanilla pod or essence

Method:

Dissolve the chocolate in the hot milk with a piece of vanilla pod. Sift together the flour, soda, baking-powder, salt and sugar. Stir in the sour cream and the butter (melted but not hot). Add the milk and chocolate mixture, after allowing it to cool and having removed the piece of vanilla pod. Fold in the lightly beaten eggs (and vanilla essence if the pod is not available, ½ teaspoon). Beat for a few minutes and then turn out into two well-greased 8″ sandwich-tins. Bake for 30 minutes in a moderate oven, 350°, Regulo 4. Sandwich together with chocolate filling, and ice if you like.

Panama Cake

This cake must be made in a tin with a loose bottom, and if possible in a spring-sided tin. It's practically impossible to turn it out of an ordinary tin without breaking it—though it can be stuck together afterwards with the filling and still taste delicious!

Ingredients: 3 eggs
2½ oz. icing sugar
2 oz. chocolate
2½ oz. almonds

Do not blanch the almonds but grate them finely or

put them through a food mill. Grate the chocolate and mix it with the almonds. Separate egg yolks and whites. Whisk egg yolks and 2 ounces of the sugar until thick and creamy.

In Austria, where this cake comes from, the cook may beat for half an hour. If you cannot face doing this you must be content with a less than perfect cake.

Whip egg whites until stiff, fold in remaining sugar, and whisk again until smooth. Fold egg whites into egg yolk mixture alternately with grated almonds and chocolate.

Bake in a buttered and floured tin in a moderate oven, 360°, Regulo 4, for about 1 hour.

When the cake is cold, cut it once or twice and fill it with the following cream:

Melt 1 ounce chocolate over hot water. Cream 2½ ounces butter with 2½ ounces icing sugar, and add the melted chocolate which should not be too hot. Beat well and then beat in an egg. Beat this mixture until it is thick and creamy.

Keep enough of the cream to cover the top and sides of the cake. Then sprinkle it with chopped, roasted almonds.

Rich Chocolate Cake

Ingredients: 8 oz. chocolate
8 oz. butter
2 oz. ground rice
6 oz. castor sugar
4 oz. flour
4 eggs
1 teaspoon baking-powder
vanilla pod or essence.
a little milk

Method:

Melt the chocolate in a little milk with a piece of vanilla pod. Cream the butter and sugar, add chocolate when cool. Separate the whites and yolks of the eggs.

Add the yolks one at a time to the butter and sugar mixture, beating each one in. Beat in the flour, rice and baking-powder, well-sieved together. Whisk the egg whites stiff and fold them in. Put the mixture into a well-greased and lined tin and bake in a moderate oven, 340°, Regulo 3, for 1¾ hours.

Gipsy Slices

Ingredients:

> 2 eggs
> 2 oz. sugar
> 2 oz. flour
> 1 oz. chocolate
> ½ oz. butter

Method:

Grate or break the chocolate and put it in a bowl with the butter. Put it in a warm place to soften. Put the eggs and sugar in a bowl over steam and whisk until thick and creamy. Remove from heat and go on beating until cool. Fold in the sieved flour, and finally the softened butter and chocolate. Put a piece of buttered greaseproof paper on to a baking-sheet, and spread the mixture on it about ½ inch thick. Bake until firm to the touch in a hot oven, 400°, Regulo 6.

Remove paper while still hot. Cut into slices when cool and fill with the following cream:

Put 2 ounces grated chocolate into a saucepan with ¼ pint cream. Bring slowly to the boil stirring all the time.

Allow to boil up once and then remove from the fire and pour into a bowl. Stir until cool. Chill thoroughly and then whisk gently until thick.

Real cream is essential and this is a most delicious filling. You can of course fill the slices with chocolate butter icing but they will not then be the genuine article.

Here are two extravagant and delicious cakes for which I give rather large quantities as they are really party pieces.

Dobos Torte

Ingredients:

>6 eggs
>5 oz. icing sugar
>4 oz. flour

Method:

Sift the flour. Separate the egg yolks and whites. Whisk the egg yolks with half the sugar until thick and creamy. Whip the egg whites until stiff and then fold in the remaining sugar. Fold the egg whites into the yolks alternately with the flour.

Spread buttered and floured cake-tins with a thin layer of the mixture. This quantity should be enough for five or six layers, and they are most easily baked in tins with removable bottoms. Remember that the filling should be as thick as the cake, so keep the layers thin! Bake in a warm oven, 380°, Regulo 5, for about 15 minutes or until pale gold.

When all the layers are cold put them one on top of the other with waxed paper in between each, cover with a board and a weight and weigh them down. Leave them like this while you prepare the filling.

For this you require:

> 4 eggs
> 4 oz. icing sugar
> 4 oz. chocolate
> 4 oz. butter
> 2 oz. ground roasted hazel nuts

Soften the chocolate in a bowl over hot water. When soft, remove from the heat, stir a little and then add the sugar and the eggs. Replace over steam and whip until thick and creamy. Remove from heat and whip until cool. Cream the butter, then add the chocolate cream, very gradually, beating in each addition really well. Finally, stir in the roasted nuts.

Now take your pastry layers from under their weight, trim them and spread them with the cream, keeping back enough to cover the sides of the cake and keeping back one pastry layer.

Place this spare round on a lightly floured board. Melt 3 oz. lump sugar over gentle heat, stirring all the time, and continue cooking until it is pale golden in colour. Remove from the fire and spread over the spare pastry round. Mark into slices with a buttered knife. This has to be done very quickly before the caramel hardens. If you find it does get hard, you can put the board with the pastry on it into a very low oven for a few seconds to soften it again.

Put this caramelled pastry on top of the other layers, and cover the sides with the remaining cream.

And here is a cake which is not cooked. It is very rich and should be served in very thin slices.

Italian Uncooked Chocolate Cake

Ingredients:

6 oz. butter
6 oz. cocoa
6 oz. ground almonds
6 oz. Petit Beurre biscuits
6 oz. sugar
1 egg
1 egg yolk
1 tablespoon very strong coffee

Method:

Melt the sugar over a very low heat in the coffee. Cream the butter and mix in the cocoa and ground almonds. Cool the sugar syrup a little and then add to the creamed mixture. Beat well. Beat the whole egg and the yolk together and stir them into the mixture. And lastly fold in the biscuits which have been broken into small pieces or roughly crumbled.

Lightly oil an oblong or square tin—a bread-tin is a good shape—and press the mixture down into it. Leave in a cold place overnight before turning out.

IV. NUT CAKES

Nut cakes are especially delicious. There are the kind most usually met with in this country with the nuts coarsely chopped and mixed into a plain cake mixture, and there are also those, more popular on the Continent, with the nuts ground finely and added to the cake in place of flour. For quite a number of these latter a cake-tin with a removable bottom is essential, as they are very delicate when warm. If you can get a tin with a spring side as well, it is an ideal piece of equipment—for these and many other cakes.

Almonds, hazel nuts and walnuts are the most popular nuts for cake-making, and though they are expensive they do add a touch of real luxury.

First, here are two of the simpler kind—a walnut cake and a hazel-nut cake. They can both be dressed up with chocolate or coffee fillings and icings, or with some of the more luscious creams given for other cakes in this chapter.

Walnut Cake

Ingredients: 4 oz. butter
9 oz. sugar
10 oz. flour
2 oz. walnuts
4 eggs
about ¼ pint milk
vanilla pod or essence
1 teaspoonful baking-powder

Method:

If you are using a vanilla pod, scald the milk with a piece of pod in it and leave it to cool with the pod still in it.

Cream the butter and the sugar together. Beat the eggs and add them to the creamed mixture alternately with the sifted flour. Beat thoroughly. Chop the walnuts and mix them in. Then add the milk after removing the vanilla pod (or add ½ teaspoon vanilla essence if you have no pod). Finally add the baking-powder.

Put the mixture into a greased and lined tin and bake in a moderate oven, 350°, Regulo 4, for 1½ hours.

Hazel Nut Cake

Ingredients: 3 oz. butter
8 oz. castor sugar
4 oz. hazel nuts
2 eggs
rind and juice of one lemon
½ lb. flour
2 teaspoonfuls baking-powder
1 teacupful milk

Method:

Put the hazel nuts on a tin in a hot oven until the skins start coming off and the nuts are slightly browned. Rub them in a teacloth to get the skins off, and then crush them or mince them coarsely.

Sieve the flour two or three times with the baking-powder.

Cream the butter and sugar together, beat in the eggs thoroughly, and then add the prepared nuts. Beat again and then stir in the flour and the grated lemon rind. Add the milk and beat again. Lastly, add the lemon juice.

Bake in a greased and lined tin for 45 to 50 minutes in a moderate oven, 350°, Regulo 4.

Semolina Almond Cake

I am putting this under nut cakes because the predominating flavour is almond. It's simple to make and rather unusual in texture.

Ingredients:

> $3\frac{1}{2}$ oz. icing sugar
> 3 eggs
> 1 oz. ground almonds
> juice and grated rind of $\frac{1}{2}$ lemon
> 2 oz. semolina

Method:

Separate the egg yolks from the whites. Add the lemon juice and the grated rind to the yolks and whisk with the sugar until thick and creamy. Beat the egg whites until stiff and then fold them into the yolk-sugar mixture alternately with the semolina and ground almonds. Bake in a buttered and floured tin in a moderate oven, 360°, Regulo $4\frac{1}{2}$.

When the cake is cool, warm some apricot jam and put it through a sieve over the cake. Then cover it with thin lemon icing.

Austrian Nusstorte

This is a really luxurious cake and makes a very good dessert.

Ingredients:
    3 eggs
    2½ oz. sugar
    2½ oz. ground walnuts
    1 oz. fine breadcrumbs
    a little rum

Method:

The breadcrumbs should be rubbed through a sieve so that they are really fine. Then put a teaspoonful of rum on them and stir them round with a fork so that the rum is evenly distributed.

Separate the egg yolks from the whites.

Whisk the yolks with the sugar until thick and creamy.

Beat the whites until stiff and fold them into the yolk-sugar mixture alternately with the breadcrumbs and the ground nuts.

Bake in a well-buttered and floured tin, with a removable bottom, in a moderate oven, 360°, Regulo 4½, for about 40 minutes.

When the cake is cool cut it twice and fill it with the following cream:

Put ¼ pint cream, 3 oz. sugar and 2 oz. ground walnuts in a saucepan and cook gently until thick. Pour into a bowl and stir until quite cool. Then beat in 3 egg yolks and a dash of rum. Whisk well.

Fill the cake with this cream and then cover it with hot, sieved jam and finally with thin lemon icing.

Nut Coffee Cake

A tin with a removable bottom is essential for this cake—unless you make small rounds of the pastry and sandwich two together with the cream, making small individual cakes. The cooked pastry keeps quite well in a tin and can be made in advance of when it is filled.

Ingredients:

       5 oz. hazel nuts or a mixture of hazel nuts
          and almonds
       5 oz. icing sugar
       3 egg whites

Method:

Blanch the hazel nuts by putting them in a hot oven for a few minutes and then rubbing them in a tea-towel to get the skins off. Blanch the almonds by pouring boiling water over them and then removing the skins.

Toast the blanched nuts lightly in the oven and then grind them finely.

Whisk the egg whites until stiff and then whisk in half the sugar. Fold in the remaining sugar and then the ground nuts.

Bake in two separate tins—or if you only have one tin available divide the mixture in two and cook first one half and then the other—in a fairly hot oven, 380°, Regulo 5, for 15 to 20 minutes—until a thin skewer comes out clean.

Handle the cooked pastry very carefully.

If you make small cakes, spread the mixture in rounds on a baking-sheet making them as nearly the same size as possible.

Sandwich them together with a coffee butter icing made as follows:

Put 3 egg yolks, 4 oz. icing sugar and 4 tablespoonfuls of strong black coffee in a bowl over steam and whisk until thick. Stir while cooling. Cream 4 oz. butter and gradually add the cold coffee cream.

Continental Hazel Nut Cake

Ingredients:

> 2½ oz. icing sugar
> 4 eggs
> 2½ oz. hazel nuts
> 1½ oz. breadcrumbs

Method:

Put the hazel nuts in a hot oven for a few minutes then rub them in a tea-towel to remove the skins. Return them to the oven for a few minutes until lightly roasted. Then grind them.

Separate the egg yolks from the whites of 3 of the eggs. Whisk the yolks and the whole egg with the sugar until very thick. Beat the egg whites stiff and fold them into the yolk mixture alternately with the ground nuts and the finely sifted breadcrumbs. Bake in a well-greased and floured tin for about 40 minutes in a moderate oven, 350°, Regulo 4.

When cold cut once or twice and fill with the following cream:

Grind 1 oz. blanched and roasted hazel nuts. Put them with a scant ½ pint milk, 2 oz. sugar, one egg and ½ oz. flour in the top of a double boiler or in a bowl over steam. Cook them until thick, stirring all the time and not allowing the mixture to get too hot. Remove from heat and stir until cold. Cream 1½ oz. butter and add the cooked mixture to it.

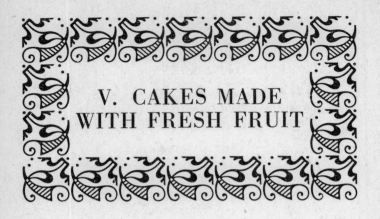

V. CAKES MADE WITH FRESH FRUIT

Plain sponges can be filled with soft fruit and cream and make delicious desserts. Cakes can also be made with the fruit cooked with them or in them or flavoured with the rind of citrus fruits. Here are two recipes for orange cakes.

Orange Cake

Ingredients:

> 4 oz. flour
> 4 oz. butter
> 4 oz. sugar
> ½ teaspoon baking powder
> 2 eggs
> grated rind of 1 orange

Method:

Cream the butter and the sugar and the grated orange rind. Sieve the flour and the baking-powder together. Separate the yolks and the whites of the eggs. Beat the yolks, one at a time, into the creamed butter mixture. Whip the whites stiff and fold them gradually into the mixture alternately with the flour.

Put the mixture into two greased sandwich-tins and bake in a moderate oven, 350°, Regulo 4, for about 15 minutes.

Sandwich together with the following filling:

Put 3 oz. cake crumbs
1 oz. butter
grated rind and juice of 1 orange
3 oz. sugar

in a saucepan. Heat gently for 5 minutes stirring all the time. Allow to cool a little and then add the yolk of one egg. Stir again over low heat until the filling thickens somewhat.

Viennese Orange Cake

Ingredients:
½ lb. icing sugar
4 egg yolks and 1 whole egg
½ lb. blanched and ground almonds—or
    other nuts
juice and grated rind of 1 orange
a handful of breadcrumbs

Method:
Butter a tin with a removable bottom and line with greased paper.

Beat the egg yolks and the whole egg with the sugar until they are very thick and creamy. Add the orange juice and grated rind and beat again thoroughly. Fold in the ground nuts and the breadcrumbs and put into the prepared tin. Bake in a moderate oven, 350°, Regulo 3½, for 45 minutes.

Remove very carefully and allow to cool before trying to take off the paper.

Warm some orange marmalade and sieve it on to the cake and spread evenly. Then cover the cake with thin orange icing.

Russian Rhubarb Cake

This is an unusual cake, good for people who like the taste of rhubarb but usually find it too sour.

Ingredients:

> 4 large eggs
> 10 oz. butter
> 12 oz. sugar
> 12 oz. flour
> 1 dessert spoon lemon juice
> ½ teaspoon cinnamon
> 2 teacups diced rhubarb
> pinch of grated nutmeg

Method:

Melt the butter without getting it very hot. Then mix all the ingredients except the rhubarb and beat vigorously. Spread the mixture over a well-greased Swiss roll tin and cover with the diced rhubarb. Sprinkle generously with sugar and bake for 45 minutes in a fairly hot oven, 400°, Regulo 6—lowering the heat slightly if cake looks like getting too brown. Cut into slices and remove them carefully with a spatula to cool on a cake-rack.

Upside down cakes are American in origin and can be

made with all kinds of fruit and nuts. Soft fruits are not suitable but stone fruits, pineapple tinned or fresh, or apples or any combination of these fruits make delicious toppings. Here is a basic recipe for:

Apple Upside Down Cake

Ingredients:
> 10 oz. flour
> 1½ teaspoons baking-powder
> 4 oz. granulated sugar
> pinch salt
> 7 oz. butter
> heaped tablespoon brown sugar
> 1 egg
> ½ cup milk
> vanilla pod or essence
> apples

Method:

Put 3 oz. butter and the brown sugar into a largish deep cake-tin and melt them together in the tin. Peel, core and skin enough apples to put a layer of apple slices in the bottom of the tin on top of the butter-sugar mixture.

Scald the milk with a piece of vanilla pod in it and allow to cool.

Sieve the dry ingredients together.

Melt the remaining 4 oz. butter without letting it get too hot.

Remove the vanilla pod from the milk and mix the milk with the well-beaten egg. (Add ½ teaspoon vanilla essence if you are not using a pod.)

Add the dry ingredients to the milk and egg and then

43

the melted butter. Beat well and pour the mixture over the apple slices in the cake-tin.

Bake in a moderate oven, 350°, Regulo 4, for about 50 minutes.

Run a knife round the side of the tin to loosen the cake and turn it over on to a hot plate. Let the cake-tin remain over it for a few minutes to allow the syrup to soak in.

Upside Down Cake can be served either hot or cold and is much improved by being served with lots of cream.

Apple Sauce Cake

This is another American cake with a very pleasant and refreshing taste.

Ingredients:

> 1 teacup unsweetened apple sauce
> 4 oz. butter
> ½ lb. sugar
> 1 egg
> 5 oz. flour
> 1 teaspoon each allspice and nutmeg
> pinch of ground cloves
> 1 teaspoon baking-powder
> pinch of salt

Method:

Sieve the dry ingredients together. Cream the butter and sugar and then beat in the egg. Stir in the apple sauce and then mix in the dry ingredients.

Bake in a well-greased large loaf-tin in a moderate oven, 350°, Regulo 4.

Ice with lemon icing when it is cool.

If you want a change from the usual fruit pie and want something that can also be eaten like a cake, you could try the following idea. It is adapted from several recipes and might perhaps be called:

Fruit Sandwich

Ingredients:

> 8 oz. flour
> 6 oz. butter
> 1 heaped tablespoon sugar
> 1 teaspoon baking-powder
> 1 egg
> 1 lemon
> fruit for filling
> a little thin cream

Method:

First prepare your fruit. Stone plums or apricots, peel and slice apples or whatever fruit you're using, and poach the fruit gently in a little water without sugar. Dried fruit is very good but of course it must be well soaked first. Allow the fruit to cool.

Now prepare your pastry. Sieve the flour with the baking-powder and mix in the sugar and the grated rind of the lemon. Rub in the fat and mix to a soft dough with the lemon juice, the egg and a little thin cream (top of the milk will do very well). You can make the cake extra delicious by substituting ground almonds for some of the flour. Line a greased sandwich-tin with half the pastry. Drain the poached fruit carefully and put it on top of the pastry. If you are using apples you can add some stoned raisins and a little cinnamon or mixed spice. With other fruit a few chopped nuts would go down very well.

Sprinkle some sugar over the fruit and then cover it with the rest of the pastry. Pinch the edges together so that they are well and truly joined and bake in a fairly hot oven, 400°, Regulo 6, about 20 minutes, until golden brown and firm to the touch. Serve with whipped cream—this makes a very pleasant dessert and can be eaten either hot or cold.

I think raspberries would make a delicious filling, but they should not be cooked first.

VI. SPICY CAKES

Spicy cakes, like fruit cakes, are good keepers. In fact some of them must be kept for at least a week in order to be at their best. If your family likes them they can be made in the last peaceful weeks before the end of term, wrapped in aluminium foil and put in a tin to be brought out when needed for holiday meals and picnics. The first recipe I'm giving is for a simple:

Gingerbread

Ingredients:

    1 breakfast-cup of black treacle
    1 breakfast-cup hot water
    1½ breakfast-cups flour
    3 oz. shortening, butter, margarine or
       lard
    1 teaspoonful bicarbonate of soda

Method:

  Put the treacle, which should be warmed, and the

water into a basin. Cut the fat into it and stir with a wire whisk until melted. Beat in the flour and finally the bicarbonate of soda. This should be a thick pouring batter.

Pour it into a greased tin with a buttered paper in the bottom (I usually use a large loaf-tin), and bake in a very moderate oven, 340°, Regulo 3, for 1 to 1½ hours, until a skewer comes out clean. Be careful it doesn't burn, and if it seems to be cooking too fast lower the heat. It is delicious eaten with butter or cream cheese.

And here is a recipe for another:

Gingerbread

This is a very good gingerbread, simple and quick to make, and as it has eggs and milk in it it is perhaps better for children.

Ingredients:

12 oz. flour
4 oz. demerara sugar
4 oz. butter
3 oz. black treacle
3 oz. golden syrup
2 eggs
¼ pint milk
1 heaped teaspoon ground ginger
1 heaped teaspoon mixed spice
1 teaspoon bicarbonate of soda

Method:

Sieve the flour and spices together. Add the sugar. Melt the butter, treacle and syrup in the milk. Add them to the flour and sugar. Add the beaten eggs. Dissolve the bicarbonate in a very little milk and beat that in as well. Pour into a well-greased loaf-tin with a piece of buttered paper in the bottom. Bake in a moderate oven, 350°, Regulo 4, for 1 to 1½ hours, until well risen and a skewer comes out clean.

Lebkuchen

This is an American-Jewish recipe and it must be kept for at least a week before eating. If you follow that rule it is delicious and rather unusual.

Ingredients:

   4 eggs
   1 lb. brown sugar
  14 oz. flour
   1 teaspoon baking-powder
   2 teaspoons cinnamon
   ¼ teaspoon allspice
   ¼ cup chopped peel
   ¼ cup chopped almonds or walnuts

Method:

Beat the eggs and sugar until thick and creamy. Sift the flour, baking-powder and spices and stir them into the egg mixture. Mix in the chopped peel and the nuts and spread about ½ inch thick on some waxed paper laid on a baking-sheet. Bake in a moderate oven, 350°, Regulo 4, for about ½ hour. Make a very thin water icing and cover the cake with this while it (the cake) is still warm. Cut into squares and store in a tin or jar with a well-fitting lid.

These quantities make a lot, but as it keeps so well, it's worth making more than you are likely to eat all at once.

Honey Cake

Ingredients:

                6 eggs, or 4 eggs plus ½ teacup coffee
                8 oz. sugar
                ¼ pint good honey
                1½ teaspoons baking-powder
                1 teaspoon bicarbonate of soda
                ½ cup each raisins and chopped nuts
                2 oz. butter, melted
            14 oz. flour
                ¼ teaspoon ground cloves
                ½ teaspoon each allspice and cinnamon
                ¼ cup chopped candied peel
                2 tablespoons brandy

Method:

Beat eggs and sugar until light and creamy. Stir in the honey and melted butter. If you use eggs and coffee dilute the honey with the hot coffee before mixing in. Sift all the dry ingredients together and add the nuts and the fruit. Mix all together, finally adding the brandy.

Turn into a well-greased and paper-lined pan (fairly shallow) and bake in a cool oven, 310°, Regulo 1½, for 1 hour.

Turn the cake in the tin upside down on to a wire rack, and allow the cake to cool before removing the tin. Cut into squares before serving. Or slice it and spread with butter.

VII. PASTRIES

Quite apart from the innumerable ways in which pastry is used there are quite a lot of different kinds. I am not including short pastry and puff pastry because recipes for these can be found in so many cookery books and experienced cooks have their own individual ideas and methods.

However, here are two tips on pastry which I have found very useful.

When I am making short pastry I start with at least double the quantities I need then and there. When I have rubbed the fat into the flour I put what I don't want immediately into the refrigerator without adding any liquid to it. Like that, it keeps for much longer than if it is made into a dough, and I can also add sugar to it if I want a sweet dough, or more butter for a richer dough, and so on. The rubbing in, which is what takes the time, can be done when I have nothing urgent to do. And then I can mix up pastry in a hurry when I need it.

The other tip is for puff pastry. Don't grease or flour your baking-sheet when you're baking puff pastry. Just sprinkle it with cold water—the pastry is not nearly so likely to be overcooked on the bottom.

Choux Pastry, from which éclairs are made, is not difficult to make, although many people seem to think it is. Here is my recipe.

Ingredients:
        ¼ pint water
        4 oz. butter
        4 oz. flour
        1 teaspoon sugar
        ¼ teaspoon salt
        4 eggs

Method:

Put the water and the butter into a pan and bring to the boil. Add the flour, sugar and salt, and stir well over heat until the mixture is dry and leaves the sides of the pan. (About 3 minutes.) Remove from the heat and add the eggs, one by one, beating each one in until it is completely absorbed. The paste should be quite smooth.

For *Chocolate Éclairs*, put the Choux pastry into a forcing bag and pipe it through a pastry tube on to a buttered and floured baking-sheet. Each éclair should be about 1 inch wide. Let them stand for about 20 minutes. Then bake for 25 to 30 minutes in a fairly hot oven, 375°, Regulo 5. They should then be golden brown and without moisture on the outside. If you take them out too soon they will collapse, though this isn't a major disaster because they can be blown up again with cream.

Fill each éclair by making a small hole in the bottom and piping in whipped cream with a pastry tube and forcing-bag. Then ice the tops with thin chocolate or coffee icing.

Cream Cheese Pastry

An extravagant but trouble-free form of puff pastry can be made with cottage cheese. I find it particularly good for meat pies and it certainly saves a great deal of work.

Take equal quantities of butter, cottage cheese and flour. Rub the butter into the flour and then work in the cheese until the whole thing forms a soft dough. Chill well before using.

A more economical version can be made by halving the quantities of butter and cheese and substituting lard. That's to say, if you have 4 oz. flour, you must have 2 oz. cheese, 2 oz. butter, 4 oz. lard.

This keeps quite well in the refrigerator if wrapped in aluminium foil.

Then there is yeast puff pastry, or Danish pastry. Perhaps this should really come in the chapter on Yeast recipes, but I think it fits in better here. There are a lot of different yeast puff pastry recipes but I find the following one very good.

Yeast Puff Pastry

Ingredients:

    5 oz. flour
    pinch of salt
    scant $\frac{1}{2}$ oz. yeast
    1 oz. melted butter
    $\frac{1}{2}$ oz. sugar
    1 large egg yolk
    scant $\frac{1}{2}$ cup milk
    3 oz. butter
    1 oz. flour

Method:

Cut the 3 oz. butter into the ounce of flour, make into a brick and chill.

Cream the yeast with the sugar and the lukewarm milk, add a little flour and put in a warm place until it starts to bubble.

Meanwhile, sift the flour with the salt into a mixing-bowl. Make a well in the centre. Drop the egg yolk into the well and add the bubbling yeast mixture. Then stir in the melted butter. If the mixture seems very wet you can add a little more flour, but the dough should be very soft, just firm enough to handle. Knead well until it is absolutely smooth. Sprinkle with a little flour, cover with a cloth and leave for 15 minutes.

Then roll it out on a floured board, making it a little thicker in the centre than at the sides. Put the butter brick in the centre and fold the sides of the pastry over it. Beat it well with the rolling-pin until it is thin enough to roll. Form it into a strip, and fold both ends to the middle. Shut it up like a book, cover with a cloth and leave in a cool place for half an hour. Repeat this rolling and folding, and then leave it in a cold place for at least 15 minutes.

You can leave the pastry overnight in a refrigerator and make *Croissants* for breakfast. Roll the pastry out to about $\frac{1}{8}''$ thickness and then cut into squares and then into triangles. Roll up the triangles with the point outside and bring down the ends to make crescents. Put on a buttered and floured baking-sheet to rise, then brush over with beaten egg, and bake in a hot oven, 390° Regulo 5½,, until golden brown.

With this puff pastry you can also make all sorts of delicious filled crescents and ring cakes. For *Filled Crescents*, make in the same way as croissants but don't cut the squares into triangles. Put a small spoonful of the filling of your choice in the centre of each square, then roll up the squares and form into crescents. Brush each one with egg and sprinkle with chopped nuts or sugar and bake in the same way as croissants.

For a *Ring Cake*, roll the pastry out into a rectangle, spread the filling of your choice over it and roll up like a swiss roll. Form into a ring and join the ends carefully. Bake in a ring pan, slashing the top of the cake several times with a sharp knife.

For fillings you can use jam, or mixtures of dried fruit, ground or chopped nuts, sugar and melted butter, bound with egg white or a little milk. You can flavour the fillings with a few drops of rum or brandy. You can add a little grated chocolate. The possibilities are as far-reaching as your ingenuity and your store cupboard will take you.

The larger cakes take a little longer to cook than the croissants so lower the heat a little when they are well risen and brown. Both sorts can be decorated, when they are cooked, with thin glacé icing.

Sweet Flan Pastry

Ingredients:

       8 oz. flour
       6 oz. butter
       1 unbeaten egg
       2 oz. sugar
       ½ teaspoon baking-powder
       ½ teacup cold milk

Method:

Rub the butter into the flour. Add the egg, sugar, baking-powder and enough milk to make a rather soft dough. Leave to stand for 15 minutes before using.

Another, rather richer, *Flan Pastry*, can be made as follows.

Ingredients:

> 5 oz. flour
> 2 oz. sugar
> 5 oz. butter
> 2½ oz. ground almonds
> few drops lemon juice
> 1 whole egg

Method:

Sift the flour and sugar together. Rub in the butter and add the almonds, the egg and the lemon juice. Knead into a dough and chill for at least an hour before using.

With this pastry you can make a delicious

Apple Flan

Line a buttered and floured sandwich-tin with the pastry and bake 'Blind' in a fairly hot oven, 380°, Regulo 5.

While it is baking, peel and slice three cooking-apples and put the slices in a pan. Add a sprinkling of sugar, a few raisins, a tablespoonful of ground almonds and a dessertspoonful of rum. Cook very gently for about 5 minutes. Allow to cool.

Put the cooked apples into the pastry-case and pipe some meringue mixture over the top in a trellis pattern.

(Make the meringue mixture by beating one white of egg stiff. Add 1 ounce castor sugar and whisk again. Finally fold in another 1½ oz. sugar.)

Put in a very cool oven, 280°, Regulo 1, until the meringue has set.

Here are two more fillings for pre-baked flan cases made with either short crust or sweet pastry.

Cheesecake

Ingredients:

> 8 oz. cottage cheese
> 3 oz. sugar
> 3 eggs
> $\frac{3}{8}$ pint milk
> 5 oz. flour
> grated rind of $\frac{1}{2}$ lemon
> 2 oz. raisins

Method:

Cream the cheese with sugar. Separate the whites and the yolks of the eggs. Beat the yolks into the cheese, add the lemon rind and gradually beat in the milk. Whip the egg whites until stiff and fold them in alternately with the flour. Pour this mixture into the flan cases and sprinkle the raisins on top. Bake in a moderate oven, 340°, Regulo 3, until well risen and golden brown.

Chocolate Chiffon Pie

Ingredients:

> 1 dessertspoonful powdered gelatine
> $\frac{3}{4}$ teacup hot water
> 2 oz. chocolate
> 6 oz. castor sugar
> 3 eggs
> pinch of salt
> $\frac{1}{8}$ pint double cream
> piece of vanilla pod or essence

57

Method:

Dissolve the gelatine in the water over a very gentle heat. Put the chocolate and the vanilla pod into a basin over boiling water until the chocolate has melted.

Separate the whites and the yolks of the eggs.

Add the egg yolks and the sugar to the melted chocolate and beat in. Cook over boiling water for 2 minutes. Remove from heat and allow to cool. Remove the vanilla pod (or if no pod add ½ teaspoonful vanilla essence).

Beat the egg whites stiff with the salt, and fold into the chocolate. Whip the cream and fold that in. Turn the mixture into the flan cases and chill till it is firm.

If you like you can omit the cream altogether, or serve it separately.

Finally, here are some 'slices' which seem to me to be nearer to pastries than either biscuits or cakes.

Linz Slices

Ingredients:

> 9 oz. flour
> 7 oz. butter
> 9 oz. sugar
> 1 egg yolk
> juice and rind of ½ lemon

Method:

Sieve the flour and sugar together. Rub in the butter. Add the egg yolk and lemon juice and grated lemon rind. Knead to a smooth dough. Roll out to ¼″ thickness, making a rectangle as near as possible.

Bake on a buttered and floured baking-sheet in a warm oven, 380°, Regulo 5, for about 20 minutes.

Cut into slices while still warm. If you want your slices really elegant then you must trim the edges of the pastry before you start cutting.

When the slices are cold, spread half of them with sweetened whipped cream, into which you have folded grated chocolate or ground roasted hazel nuts. For the quantity of pastry given above you'll need ¼ pint cream. Put the other slices on top and dust with icing sugar.

Bee Sting Slices

Ingredients:

> 9 oz. flour
> 7 oz. butter
> 1½ oz. sugar
> 3 tablespoons milk
> 3½ oz. vanilla sugar
> 2 oz. ground almonds
> pinch of baking-powder

Method:

Sieve the flour, the 1½ oz. sugar (not the vanilla sugar) and baking-powder together. Rub in half the butter and make into a dough with the milk. Cover with a cloth and leave.

Melt the rest of the butter over a very low heat. Stir in the ground almonds and vanilla sugar and go on stirring until the mixture is quite smooth. Take off the heat and stir until cool.

Roll out the dough ¼" thick, making it as rectangular as possible. Put it on a buttered and floured baking-sheet. Spread the almond mixture over it and bake for about 35 minutes in a moderate oven, 350°, Regulo 4. Cut into slices when cold.

Metternich Slices

Ingredients:

> 1 lb. flour
> 4 oz. butter
> 4 egg yolks
> 1 tablespoon cream
> 1 tablespoon rum

Method:

Sieve the flour. Rub in the butter. Make into a dough with the egg yolks, the cream and the rum.

Roll it out very thin and trim it round the edges to make a rectangle. Put it on a buttered and floured baking-sheet. Spread it thinly with apricot jam and use the pastry trimmings to make a trellis over the jam. Brush it over with egg yolk and bake in a warm oven, 380°, Regulo 5 until golden brown.

Cut into slices when cold.

VIII. BISCUITS

It's a good idea to make more biscuits than you need any one time. They keep well in a tin and are useful for snacks.

Ginger Wafers

Ingredients:

> 6 oz. flour
> 2 oz. black treacle
> 2 oz. butter
> 2 oz. soft brown sugar
> 1 teaspoon ground ginger
> $\frac{1}{2}$ teaspoon baking-powder

Method:

Melt the butter, the sugar and the treacle over a low heat until well blended, but the mixture must not get very hot. Sieve the dry ingredients and mix them with the treacle mixture to form a stiff paste. Roll out very thin—but do not try to roll out more than a small quantity at a time. The paste is very difficult to handle when it gets cold, and if you find it's getting too brittle, return it to the saucepan and warm very gently until it gets soft again. Cut into rounds and bake in a very moderate oven, 340°, Regulo 3.

Chocolate Biscuits

Ingredients:

      8 oz. sugar
      4 oz. butter
      3 oz. chocolate
      2 eggs
   10 oz. flour
      ½ teaspoon salt
      ¾ teaspoon bicarbonate of soda
      vanilla pod or 1 teaspoon vanilla essence

Method:

Put the chocolate and the piece of vanilla pod in a bowl over hot water to melt. Cream the butter and sugar. Add the melted chocolate after allowing it to cool slightly and having removed the vanilla pod. Add the eggs (and the vanilla essence if you have no pod). Sift the dry ingredients and add to the mixture and mix until quite smooth. Chill well and then roll out about ⅛″ thick. Cut with a knife or with biscuit-cutters and place on a greased baking-sheet and bake for 10 minutes in a warm oven, 375°, Regulo 4½.

This mixture is also suitable for using with a biscuit-press. But in this case, do not grease the baking-sheet and bake at a slightly lower temperature (350°, Regulo 4), as they will be rather thick and will take longer to cook.

Rich Flapjacks

There are a lot of recipes for these rolled oat biscuits. This one, which is rather extravagant, is especially good.

Ingredients:

> 6 oz. butter
> 6 oz. demerara sugar
> 8 oz. rolled oats
> pinch of salt

Method:
Cream the butter. Mix the sugar, the oats and the salt together and stir them into the butter. Make sure they are well blended and then turn the mixture into a swiss roll-tin. Smooth it down with a spatula or palette-knife. Bake in a hot oven, 425°, Regulo 7, for about 30 minutes. Leave in the tin until cooled a little and then mark into squares with a knife. When quite cold, cut into squares and remove from tin.

Coffee Sandwich Biscuits

Ingredients:

> 3 oz. flour
> 1 oz. ground rice
> 3 oz. butter
> 2 oz. castor sugar
> 2 teaspoons instant coffee
> 1 teaspoon water
> halved walnuts (if you like)

Method:
Sieve the flour and ground rice together. Cream the

butter and sugar. Mix the coffee with the water and beat into the creamed butter and sugar. Fold in the dry ingredients and mix together. Roll out thin and cut into rounds—if you use walnuts, put half a walnut on every other biscuit.

Put them on a greased baking-sheet and bake in a moderate oven, 350°, Regulo 4, for about 15 minutes. Cool on a wire rack.

When they're cold put them together with the following cream:

Cream 1 oz. butter with 2 oz. icing sugar and then beat in 1 teaspoon instant coffee mixed with 1 teaspoon cream.

Chocolate Brownies

Ingredients:

       3 oz. plain chocolate
       3 oz. shelled walnuts
       3 oz. butter
       3 oz. sugar
       1 egg
       4 oz. flour
       $\frac{1}{4}$ teaspoon baking-powder
       $\frac{1}{4}$ teaspoon salt
       piece of vanilla pod or 1 teaspoon vanilla
          essence
       a little milk

Method:

Melt the chocolate with the piece of vanilla pod in a bowl over hot water.

Chop the walnuts.

Cream the butter and sugar. Add the beaten egg gradually, beating it in well. Sift the flour, salt and baking-powder together and stir into the mixture. Remove the vanilla pod from the melted chocolate which should not be too hot. Add the chocolate and the nuts (and the vanilla essence if you have no pod) to the other ingredients. If necessary add a little milk to make a soft batter.

Bake in a well-greased rectangular tin about 8″ square in a moderate oven, 350°, Regulo 4, for about 25 minutes. Be careful not to overbake. Leave in the tin to cool and cut into squares while still warm.

Shortbread

Ingredients:

> 6 oz. flour
> 2 oz. ground rice or fine semolina
> 5 oz. butter
> 2 oz. sugar
> level teaspoon salt

You can of course use margarine instead of butter, but if you want the authentic shortbread flavour then you must use butter.

Method:

Sieve the dry ingredients together and then work in the butter. Go on kneading until the whole thing forms a pliable dough. When quite smooth either form into one round cake about ½″ thick or cut into small ones. Prick the surface with a fork. Bake in a moderate oven, 350°, Regulo 4, on a greased and floured baking-sheet until pale golden brown.

If you have a wooden shortbread mould, flour it well and press the dough into it. Take a sharp knife and run it over the surface of the dough so that it is quite smooth and there is none sticking to the rim of the mould. Then bang the side of the mould sharply on the table while turning the mould round so that the dough is loosened from the side. Finally turn it on to the baking-sheet, keeping one hand on the dough to prevent it from breaking. If it sticks the first time do not despair but take out all the dough, flour the mould again and repeat the process. The butter from the dough will have oiled the mould and should make it turn out all right. The dough is much less likely to break if it is warm from being kneaded, so if it seems very brittle work it some more with your hands.

Vanilla Crescents

Icing sugar, flavoured with a vanilla pod, is essential for these biscuits to taste really good, though they would be quite nice coated with ordinary icing sugar.

Ingredients:

> 1 oz. almonds
> 2 oz. sugar
> vanilla sugar
> 3 oz. butter
> 4 oz. flour

Method:

Grind the almonds without blanching them. Sieve the flour and sugar together. Add the ground almonds. Rub the butter into the dry ingredients. Knead into a smooth paste. Take small bits of dough and roll them between your hands, then form into crescents. Bake on a greased and floured baking-sheet in a warm oven, 380°, Regulo 5, until dark golden brown. Roll in the vanilla sugar while still hot.

Austrian Biscuits

Ingredients:

> 4 oz. butter
> 6 oz. flour
> 6 oz. sugar
> 6 oz. almonds
> 1 oz. grated chocolate
> 1 egg or 2 egg yolks
> pinch of cinnamon
> pinch of nutmeg

Method:

Grind the almonds without blanching them. Mix them and all the other dry ingredients together. Rub in the butter. Make into a dough with the egg and go on kneading until it is very smooth. Roll out to $\frac{1}{8}''$ thickness and cut with a biscuit-cutter. Put on a greased and floured baking-sheet and brush with egg white and sprinkle with ground almonds. Bake in a moderate oven, 380°, Regulo 5, until brown—about 15 minutes.

Orange Jumbles

Ingredients:

> 4 oz. castor sugar
> ¼ lb. almonds
> 3 oz. butter
> 3 oz. flour
> juice of 2 oranges
> grated rind of 1 orange

Method:

Blanch the almonds and shred them. Cream the butter

and sugar together with the grated orange rind. Then mix in the flour, the shredded almonds and the orange juice. Drop the mixture in teaspoonfuls on to a greased baking-sheet leaving plenty of room for them to spread. Bake in a moderate oven, 350°, Regulo 4, for about 10 minutes. Allow them to cool a little before lifting with a palette-knife on to a rack to cool.

Biscuits of similar texture but with a chocolate flavour are:

Chocolate Fondant Biscuits

Ingredients:

> 7 oz. sugar
> 5 oz. butter
> 5 oz. chocolate
> 5 oz. almonds
> 1 tablespoon flour
> glacé cherries (if you like)

Method:

Do not blanch the almonds but put them on a tin in a hot oven for a few minutes until they are lightly roasted. Then grind them.

Melt the chocolate in a bowl over hot water. Cream the butter and sugar, then add the flour, ground almonds and melted chocolate which should not be too hot.

Put teaspoonfuls of the mixture on to a greased and floured baking-sheet leaving plenty of room for them to spread. Flatten them slightly with a knife and decorate with halved glacé cherries if you like. Bake in a hot oven, 400°, Regulo 6, for about 10 minutes. Remove carefully with a palette-knife while still hot.

If you have been making mayonnaise or some other recipe which only requires the yolks of eggs you might like some ideas for using up the whites. Meringues are the obvious answer, but there are a lot of other recipes which are a bit more unusual. For instance, there are those delicious little wafers which go well with stewed fruit or ice-cream:

Cat's Tongues

Ingredients:

> 2 oz. butter
> 2 oz. castor sugar
> 2 egg whites
> 2 oz. plain flour

Method:

Warm the butter so that it is soft but not oily. Beat it lightly with a fork or wire whisk and gradually add the sugar, beating all the time until it is light and fluffy.

Do not whisk the egg whites but beat them very gradually into the butter and sugar, a very little at a time. Sieve the flour with a pinch of salt and fold it carefully in. You can flavour with grated lemon rind or use vanilla flavoured sugar, if you like.

Pipe the mixture through a plain $\frac{1}{2}''$ tube into $2''$ lengths on to a greased and floured baking-sheet. Allow room for the tongues to spread.

Bake in a hot oven, 400°, Regulo 6, for about 6 minutes until they are golden brown round the edges.

Or there are:

Hazel Nut Macaroons

Ingredients:

      2 egg whites
      3 oz. castor sugar
      2 oz. hazel nuts—after the skins have
          been removed

Method:

Put a good 2 oz. hazel nuts into a hot oven until the nuts are slightly toasted and the skins come off easily. Put them in a tea-towel and rub off the skins. Then grind them.

Whisk the egg whites until stiff. Whisk in half the sugar and then fold in the rest of the sugar alternately with the ground hazel nuts.

Either drop teaspoonfuls of the mixture on to a greased and floured baking-sheet or pipe them into small mounds. Bake in a cool oven, 320°, Regulo 2, until they are just coloured—about 1 hour.

English Biscuits

This recipe was given me by an Austrian friend who told me they are called Englander Backerei. I can't imagine anything less English.

Ingredients:

             4 whites of eggs
             8 oz. icing sugar
             8 oz. almonds
             1 lemon

Method:

Blanch and chop the almonds. Beat the egg whites until stiff. Fold in the sugar, the almonds and the grated rind of the lemon. Stir in the juice of the lemon, and then put the mixture in a bowl over hot water. Beat over steam until the mixture thickens. Drop teaspoonfuls of the mixture on to rice paper laid on a baking-sheet and dry the biscuits in a very cool oven, 280°, Regulo 1.

A similar mixture can be made omitting the lemon rind and juice and substituting 3 oz. chopped mixed peel for 3 oz. of the almonds, and reducing the amount of sugar to 5 oz.

The result is called *Widow's Kisses!*

IX. YEAST CAKES

There is no special difficulty in making cakes with yeast. They are economical, and yeast will keep well if kept in a cold place and wrapped in waxed paper. The only thing they require more of than ordinary cakes is time. However, the first recipe needs less of that than most yeast recipes because it only has to rise once. It is called:

Semolina Yeast Cake

Ingredients:

> 2 oz. semolina
> 8 oz. flour
> 2 oz. sugar
> grated rind of 1 orange
> ½ oz. yeast
> 3 oz. butter
> 2 eggs
> 2 oz. currants
> milk

and for the top 2 oz. flour
            2 oz. sugar
            2 oz. butter
            2 teaspoons cinnamon
            jam

Method:

Cream the yeast with a teaspoonful of sugar and 3 tablespoons warm milk and leave in a warm place until it bubbles.

Meanwhile, mix the semolina, the flour and the sugar together. Rub in the butter. Stir in the bubbling yeast mixture, add the eggs beaten up with 2 tablespoons milk. Finally add the grated orange rind and the currants.

Turn into a greased loaf-pan and add the top mixture as follows. First spread some jam over the top of the cake (it's easier to spread if warmed slightly). Then rub the flour, the sugar, the cinnamon and the butter together until the mixture is crumbly, and sprinkle this on top of the jam.

Leave the cake to rise in a warm place for about half an hour or until doubled in size. Bake in a fairly hot oven, 400°, Regulo 6, for about 40 minutes.

Oven Baked Doughnuts

Fried doughnuts are a nuisance to cook and very hot work. These jam-filled buns are baked and not fried and are very light and delicious.

Ingredients:
            1 lb. flour
            2 eggs
            2 oz. sugar

pinch of salt
4 oz. butter
½ oz. yeast
about ⅜ pint milk
grated rind of 1 lemon
jam
melted butter for brushing over the buns

Method:

Melt the butter but do not allow it to get hot. Cream the yeast with a teaspoon of sugar and a little flour (about a teaspoonful). Warm the milk a little and add half a teacupful to the creamed yeast—then leave it in a warm place until it bubbles.

Sift the flour and salt together and make a well in the centre. Into this pour the eggs which have been whisked together with the sugar, the rest of the milk and the melted butter. Then add the lemon rind and the yeast mixture.

Beat everything with a wooden spoon until it leaves the side of the bowl. Add a little flour if the mixture seems to be too wet, but be careful not to add too much. The mixture should be just firm enough to handle.

Dust the top of the dough with a little flour and cover with a cloth. Leave to rise for 1 hour.

Butter and flour a swiss roll tin.

Roll out the dough on a floured board to about ¼″ thickness. As the dough is very soft you may find it easier to pat it and pull it to the required thickness. Then cut into 2½″ squares. Dab some jam into the centre of each square and fold the corners together. Pinch them firmly so that the jam is sealed inside.

Have some melted butter in a saucer and taking each bun in turn, put it lightly into the butter and brush some butter all over the bun. As each bun is buttered put it into the swiss roll tin with the pinched-together corners underneath. The buns should touch each other when in the tin. When they are all in, brush them all over with a little more butter, then cover with a cloth and leave them to rise in a warm place for 30 minutes.

Bake in a warm oven, 380°, Regulo 5, until golden brown—about 20 minutes. Turn on to rack to cool. They will be joined together but when cold they can be separated and should then be sprinkled with icing sugar.

There are, of course, hundreds of ways of making sweet yeast doughs, which can then be used to make buns and cakes. The following recipe is very good and the result is perhaps more like cake in texture than some.

Sour Cream Dough

Ingredients:

> 6 oz. butter
> 6 oz. sugar
> 3 eggs
> 1 teacup sour cream
> 1 lb. 6 oz. flour (about)
> grated rind of 1 lemon
> 1 oz. yeast
> a little warm milk
> 1 teaspoonful salt

Method:

Dissolve the yeast in 2 tablespoonfuls of warm milk. Cream the butter and the sugar, then add the beaten eggs, the sour cream, the lemon rind and the yeast mixture. Mix this all well together as you add the different

75

ingredients, and then add the flour sifted with the salt. Knead the mixture really well.

If you haven't got a wide bowl, then put the dough on a floured board or table-top so that you can turn it over and over and pummel it with your hands. Go on kneading until the dough is absolutely smooth and the surface is satiny.

Put the dough back in the bowl, dust it with flour, cover the bowl with a damp cloth and leave overnight in a warm room. In the morning you can use the dough for a number of different buns and cakes.

For small buns, pinch off pieces of dough. Flatten them to about $\frac{1}{2}''$ thickness, then put some sweet filling on each bun, pull up the corners and pinch them together. Put them, join side down, on a baking-sheet. Slash the tops with a sharp-pointed knife so that the filling shows through. Brush them with egg yolk and leave them to rise until they are light and puffy. Bake for 10 to 15 minutes in a warm oven, 375°, Regulo $4\frac{1}{2}$.

Or, you can roll out a large piece of the dough—about half the given quantity—and spread some filling over the surface, and roll up like a swiss roll. Either join the ends of the roll together to make a ring, or curve into a horse-shoe shape. Slash the top several times, brush over with egg yolk and prove in the same way as the buns. Bake in the same oven heat for 10 minutes, then lower the heat a little and bake for another 20 minutes or so.

Here are some suggestions for fillings which can be used in the same way with other sweet doughs.

Mix equal quantities of cakecrumbs and ground nuts, moisten with rum or brandy. Spread over the dough then sprinkle with sugar and cinnamon. Finally drizzle melted butter over the whole surface.

To this sort of mixture you can add a little grated chocolate, dried fruits of all kinds, warmed honey instead of the sugar, grated lemon or orange rind, ground poppy seeds—anything you think might be nice.

If you are making fillings for small buns then they must of course be fully mixed before filling the buns—otherwise you'll get into difficulties sprinkling sugar and melted butter, etc.

Or, you could use your dough to make a *Fresh Fruit Yeast Cake*.

Roll out the dough into a neat rectangle and put on to a buttered and floured baking-sheet. Cover the surface of the dough with slices of apples, plums cut in half (stoned and put cut surface uppermost on the dough), or stoned cherries. Leave to rise covered with a cloth until the edge of the dough feels springy.

Meanwhile, rub together 1 oz. butter, 2½ oz. flour, 1 oz. sugar and 1 oz. ground almonds until they are crumbly. Add a few drops of milk, or a little egg white, and spread this mixture over the fruit—it should be quite thickly spread.

Bake in a warm oven, 390°, Regulo 5½, for about half an hour, lowering the heat a little when the cake begins to brown round the edges. Allow to cool a little after baking and then sprinkle thickly with icing sugar.

Cut into slices before serving.

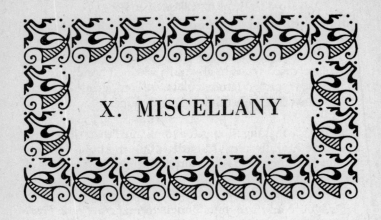

X. MISCELLANY

In this chapter I have put the cakes which didn't seem to fit into any of the other categories or which I hadn't made until after the other chapters had been typed.

The first is a luxury party cake which is not baked but chilled in the refrigerator. It sounds very extravagant but it is very rich and only the very greedy would eat a lot of it!

Rum and Coffee Cake

This is best made in a cake-tin with a removable bottom, but it can be made on a flat dish—in which case it cannot be weighted while it chills and will therefore be more difficult to cut.

Ingredients:
> 3 dozen sponge finger biscuits (approx.)
> 3 oz. hazel nuts or almonds or a mixture
>   of both
> ½ cup hot milk

3 oz. butter
3 oz. icing sugar
2 egg yolks
a little rum
about ½ pint strong black coffee (or
    coffee and milk)

Method:

Blanch the almonds, if used. Toast the nuts in a hot oven and grind them. With hazel nuts the skins should be rubbed off in a tea-towel before grinding. Pour the ½ cup of hot milk over the ground nuts and leave to cool.

Cream the butter with the icing sugar and then gradually beat in the egg yolks. Add the nut and milk mixture and mix lightly but well. Butter a cake-tin. Put the black coffee (cold), or the coffee and milk, into a soup plate and add rum to taste—about a teaspoonful is probably enough for most people. Now dip the finger biscuits one at a time into the coffee so that the outside is soft but they are still crisp inside. Line the bottom of the cake-tin with these. You cannot hope to cover the bottom completely but by breaking the biscuits into thirds you can put a ring round the outside and then fill in the centre with whole biscuits and smaller pieces. Cover them with a layer of the nut cream, then put down another layer of dipped biscuits, then another layer of the cream and finish with a final layer of biscuits.

Butter the bottom of a plate, which will fit inside the tin, put it butter-side down on top of the cake and weight it down. Chill overnight, if possible, and certainly for several hours.

Push the cake out very carefully, and then cut some sponge fingers the same height as the cake, and stick them round the outside. You can tie them on with a ribbon.

Cover the top of the cake with whipped cream.

You can omit the sponge fingers round the outside and the whipped cream—and the ribbon!

If you make the cake on a dish do not attempt to weight it. But it must be thoroughly chilled. It'll taste just as good as the one from the cake-tin, but it will be more messy to cut.

Mozart Cake

This is rather like an extraordinarily good shortbread with chocolate icing on top.

Ingredients:
- ½ lb. butter
- ½ lb. sugar
- ½ lb. nuts
- 1 whole egg and 1 yolk
- grated rind of 1 lemon
- 4 oz. flour
- a good pinch each of nutmeg, cinnamon and ground cloves

Method:

Grind the nuts which should not be blanched.

Sift the flour with the spices.

Cream the butter with the sugar and the grated lemon rind. Beat the egg and the yolk together and beat them into the creamed mixture. Then fold in the flour and the ground nuts.

Butter and flour a cake-tin (with a removable bottom if possible) and put in the mixture and bake in a moderate oven, 350°, Regulo 4. When cold ice with chocolate icing.

Easter Sponge Cake

Ingredients:

>4 eggs
>the weight of 4 eggs in icing sugar
>the weight of 3 eggs in ground almonds
>the weight of 1 egg in flour

Method:

Separate the whites and the yolks of the eggs.

Beat the yolks with the sugar until they are pale in colour and very thick.

Whip the whites quite stiff.

Sift the flour and add it to the ground almonds.

Fold the egg whites alternately with the flour and almonds into the egg yolk mixture.

Put into a buttered and floured tin and bake in a moderate oven, 350°, Regulo 4.

Remove from the tin and when cold cut it twice and fill with a really good chocolate butter icing.

Spread the top of the cake with slightly warmed redcurrant jelly and then ice with thin chocolate icing.

Lastly, here is a lovely Austrian cake called:

Muerbe Torte

Ingredients:

>5 oz. flour
>5 oz. butter
>2 hard-boiled egg yolks
>grated rind of $\frac{1}{2}$ lemon
>2 oz. icing sugar
>jam

Method:

Sieve the egg yolks with the flour and the sugar. Cut the butter into these, grate in the lemon rind, and rub in the butter until a dough is formed. Divide it into two or three, depending on what size you want your cake to be, and make each section into a round flat cake. If you use a cake-tin as a guide it's fairly easy to make them the same size.

Put the rounds on to a buttered and floured baking-sheet and bake them in a fairly hot oven, 380°, Regulo 5, for 15 to 20 minutes.

When they're cold sandwich them together with jam and dust the top with icing sugar.

XI. ICINGS AND FILLINGS

I am no good at decorative icing but I never think it matters if home-made cakes are not elaborately iced. A plain icing looks much better than a bad attempt at decoration, and very often a good cake is spoiled by the excessive sweetness of the icing if too much is put on in an effort to make it look nice.

Glacé Icing

The simplest form of glacé icing is sieved icing sugar mixed with water. Very little water is needed but the mixture should only just coat the back of a spoon. Stand your cake on a rack and pour the icing over it. Some is bound to run off if the icing is of the right consistency, so dip a knife in hot water and run it round the sides of the cake to spread the icing as it runs down.

To make a better surface on the cake before applying glacé icing, cover the cake with slightly warmed red currant jelly, or apricot jam which has been put through a sieve.

To flavour glacé icing you can use orange or lemon juice instead of water to mix with the icing sugar. Or you can use rum, maraschino or other liqueurs, or coffee, all of them diluted with water according to taste.

To make chocolate glacé icing, melt some chocolate in a little water and when it is quite smooth mix it with sieved icing sugar. A nut of butter beaten in gives a good gloss.

It's very difficult to give exact quantities, as icing sugar varies, but I'm sure it's better to err on the side of thinness. You can put a plate under the rack on which the cake is standing so that you can scrape up the icing if too much runs down. You'll be surprised how much remains on the cake even when the icing seems much too thin.

Still, the whole art of making glacé icing can really only be learned by experience.

American Frosting

Ingredients:

> 1 lb. granulated sugar
> ¼ pint water
> 2 egg whites

Method:

Put the sugar and the water over low heat and stir until the sugar has completely dissolved. Bring to the boil and heat until it reaches 238°, or until a little dropped into cold water immediately makes a soft ball.

Whisk the egg whites stiff and pour the syrup slowly on to them, whisking all the time.

This icing can be flavoured with orange or lemon rind, instant coffee or liqueurs. American frosting can also be used as a filling.

Fillings

The simplest filling is, of course, jam; the most delicious is whipped cream, either alone or mixed with other things.

You might like to try some of the following:

a cake sandwiched together or topped with whipped cream covered by a layer of fresh fruit or tinned fruit well drained of syrup;

whipped cream into which is folded grated chocolate or nuts (which have been lightly toasted before grating);

sweetened whipped cream mixed with a dash of strong black coffee, or rum or other liqueurs.

More elaborate fillings can be made from variations of:

Butter Icing

Basically this is butter and sugar creamed together in the proportions of 3 oz. butter to 4 to 6 oz. icing sugar.

The simplest ways of flavouring this are with vanilla, orange or lemon rind, instant coffee or a little cocoa. It should be very well beaten so that it is light and fluffy.

Chocolate butter icing is made in the same way, but after the butter and sugar have been creamed add 1 oz. of melted chocolate—this should be quite soft but not hot.

All these butter icings are made more delicious by adding an egg yolk, or well-beaten whole egg. It should be beaten in gradually after the butter and sugar have been creamed.

Other butter icings can be made as follows.

Chocolate Nut Icing—To chocolate butter icing add 1 egg and 1 oz. of toasted and grated hazel nuts or almonds.

Coffee Cream Filling—Whisk 3 egg yolks with 4 tablespoons strong black coffee and 4 oz. icing sugar over steam until thick. Cream 4 oz. butter and then beat in the coffee cream a teaspoonful at a time.

Vanilla Cream—Whisk 2 egg yolks, ½ teacup cream and a pinch of flour over steam until thick. Cream 3 oz. butter with 3 oz. vanilla sugar (or plain icing sugar and a few drops of vanilla essence). Add the egg yolk mixture gradually, beating all the time.

Finally, here is an idea to lift a plain cake into the luxury class.

Punch Filling

Cut a plain sponge or madeira cake into three layers. Set the bottom and top layers on one side after spreading the cut surfaces with jam.

Cut the middle layer into cubes. Put 3 oz. granulated sugar, grated rind and juice of 1 orange, ⅛ pint water, 2 tablespoonfuls rum into a saucepan. Add a few drops of maraschino—which can be omitted. Bring to the boil and pour over the cake cubes. Mix in 1 tablespoonful apricot jam and stir well.

Now sandwich the other two layers together with the Punch mixture.

You can, of course, use a bought cake for this treatment. And if you ice it with orange glace icing you will get all the credit!

Index